White Label Digital Marketing
Brittany Filori & Michael Borgelt

Acknowledgments

We would like to thank all of our mentors and teachers that have helped shape the journey in our marketing careers. To our fellow peers for challenging us to step outside our own ideas each day, to Google for always keeping us on our toes, and most importantly thank you to those reading this book who are serving other small businesses in the community. Helping you continue to see success in your own agency is a big part of why we wrote this book. Our passion to help grow companies (both large and small) is at the root of everything we do at 51Blocks. We're so excited to share this process with you. Enjoy!

CHAPTERS

ONE

White Label Overview

"Start with the end in mind. " — *Stephen R. Covey,*
The 7 Habits of Highly Effective People

For many Owners, they are not thinking about their end goal at this moment. They are thinking about how to simply get through their day. As an agency owner you face pressure from all sides to ensure the machine you built is well-oiled and viable as your path for time and financial freedom in the future.

What if you could shortcut this path? Rather than juggling the daily struggles of being an owner, strategist, manager, marketer and the other 30 hats you wear to run your company - what if you could hire a team to handle everything from onboarding through management, strategy, fulfillment and communication so you could focus on growth and sales?

You are in a business that has been built to grow your client's businesses. However, how do you ensure the growth of your own company? White label partnerships are an invaluable resource that your company needs to capitalize on to ensure that it increases its margins. Hiring an agency partner puts the right people in the right seats to serve your business as an extension of your team so you can move away from managing people and clients to focus on scaling towards your goals.

How many times have you envisioned the day where you can play golf or spend time with your loved ones more often then you're working? How about the financial security to collect checks without dealing with all those headaches from the day-to-day? Many of the agency owners who come to 51Blocks tell us of these visions and dreams. Our solution is to provide a turnkey solution that turns these thoughts into reality.

Most of you who are reading this book probably already have a good idea of what a white label partner is and does. We're going to walk you through the ins and outs of how to establish and build a quality partnership. If you're new to this concept, here's a quick overview of the basics when it comes to what companies like ours do for businesses like yours.

White Label Definition

"White label" refers to the outsourcing of work to another company while you keep your brand name on all the work that gets done for you. To be more specific, you have another company handling fulfillment for your company while you reap the benefits. This move will, in the long run, increase your potential profit since your client will not have to look elsewhere to get the work done, and you get to keep that business.

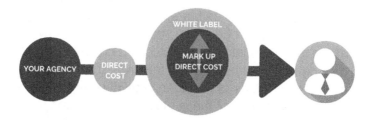

Would you be willing to raise your prices for a better quality product and reputation?

Qualities of a Successful White Label Partnership

We've met a lot of owners over a decade. From those who are hoping to start their own agency in the future all the way to the seasoned digital marketing professional. Below are the qualities of the owners who came in with an open mind and clear vision. We've found that these shared values between partners make for the most fruitful partnership.

Collaboration - The only way to make a successful partnership work is to maintain a collaborative spirit throughout the process. Teamwork is the core skill everyone should have as two agencies become one. You should be prepared for some growing pains, but know your partner will do what it takes to remedy those quickly.

Strategic Planning - Whether you're allowing your partner to take care of the strategy, collaboratively strategizing, or simply allocating tasks - this stage is essential to do together. The more information shared, the better for all. Stay organized with your partner for optimal success.

Communication & Synergy - Throughout this process you're going to have highs and lows in the campaign. Open communication with your team and client will help keep the team's synergy to be a united front under one umbrella. This is where transparency is key.

Performance - Reporting on the performance of the campaign KPIs each month is essential in retaining your clients, showing them the value of the service along with ROI and for you to see the performance of your partner. Elevate your team here to showcase the ROI you've brought to your client through the team's strategy and wins.

Success - Achieving success with your clients is the job of your partner, but being able to effectively use white labeling as a way to scale your agency will be where you see your own success.

Chapter One Reflection

What are my top 3 reasons for white labeling?

    1. _____

    2. _____

    3. _____

What are some of my initial questions about partnerships I'm hoping this book will answer?

    1. _____

    2. _____

    3. _____

What are the most important qualities to me for a partnership to work?

    1. _____

    2. _____

    3. _____

TWO

Scaling Your Agency

Growing an agency to the next level is like playing a game of tetris. You might not always fit everything together perfectly, but it's a strategic game of knowing how to make your way to the top - one piece at a time. Have you identified which piece is holding you back from scaling? The ideal white label partnership will fit into your agency seamlessly as that final piece to get you to the next level.

Is My Company Ready to Scale?

Are you wondering if your company is scalable? You will need to take a look at your overall business to determine if your offering is viable to scale. Ask yourself what you would need to meet an increase in demand. Scaling is only possible when you are able to increase your output of products without increasing your input investment for fulfilling the output demands. For example; if you can sign that new client and fill their order without having to invest in more employees.

For scalability to be an option, your company should have recurring revenue, consistent recurring customers, have a diverse income, and have the connections or partners to help you achieve success. When you are considering scaling, you may want to look into a white label partnership to help you achieve your goals. You need to have a business plan mapped out and a digital marketing plan that can help you carry out your business plan.

Scaling Together

Having a white label partner will give you the benefit of their marketing expertise without the need to hire a new employee to complete the task. You will also be gaining the insight they can bring, about what works and what does not in the digital marketing process. Your white label partnership could become the answer you need to make your scaling dreams a reality.

What does it mean to scale? Your reasons were likely defined in the Chapter One Reflection. For most this will center around time & financial freedom.

Choosing The Right Partner

You want to make sure that your collaboration fulfills your needs and that your partner has the experience needed to take your ideas and make them a reality.

So what should you be looking for in a white label partnership? You want a partner that has experience in digital marketing that can bring an understanding of the best practices for marketing success. You also want a partner that will communicate with you throughout the whole process and explain their methods and procedures. Finally, make sure that the partnership you choose will listen to your concerns and work with you instead of for you.

Working Towards a Common Goal

Your goal is to get a company that has the experience to help you achieve your goals and more. With a proven process of assessing your companies needs and the knowledge to use the proper channels to fulfill those needs, the scaling process will be efficient and successful. This experience for success is what a white label partnership can bring to your company.

With a tried and true process, you'll collaboratively use your experience to help you achieve your company's goals. Our process starts with communication and transparency. Whether the white label partners are communicating with you or directly with your client, they will make sure that you know what is being done and why. That's why each one of our partners here at 51Blocks gets the personal attention that they deserve and an individualized plan to fit their needs and goals.

White Label Partnership Checklist

Unsure of what type of white label relationship your agency needs? Partnerships come in all different forms. The three main types are:

1. **Full Service** (onboarding through strategic development and client management)
2. **Strategic Partnership** (may or may not be client facing, but you rely on this team to develop strategy and execute accordingly)
3. **Fulfillment Only** (you delegate tasks to the fulfillment team who executes and reports)

Which one is right for you?

Define what seats in your company are missing or determine where you need the most relief and walk through the checklist below to find out what will suit you best.

Yes	Sometimes	No	I'm looking for...
1	2	3	A partner who can help me onboard my clients.
1	2	3	A partner who can do a deep dive and develop a complete strategy for my client's campaigns.
1	2	3	A partner who can compliment my own team and represent my agency

			client-facing.
1	2	3	A partner who will be fulfilling all tasks as outlined in the strategy.
1	2	3	A partner who can conduct client meetings as handle all client emails for the campaign.
1	2	3	A partner who has a complete management structure internally who can handle client fires.
1	2	3	A partner who provides monthly reporting that I can use client-facing.
1	2	3	A partner who provides sales support with custom quotes that fit within my current service offerings.
1	2	3	A partner who will help me develop packages to sell to my clients.
1	2	3	A partner who can have weekly team meetings so I have a complete understanding of the campaign.
1	2	3	I'm not interested in being a part of the client management and I just want to sell.

Mostly 1's - You're probably an agency with 5 or less employees or you're new to digital marketing and need an all-in-one solution. Your ideal partnership is one where you sell, and the white label partner takes care of your client from onboarding through day-to-day management. You'll want to find a partner who has a strong internal structure for overall client success and happiness as they'll be a big part of your own agency's reputation. You're looking for complete fulfillment.

Mostly 2's - You're a mid-size agency that needs a partner to help with your current team's efforts. Whether complimenting them or being an extension of your agency, you need your white label partnership to be flexible based on the client. Finding an agency that is great at communication and collaboration is going to be important as you might not need them in the same way for each client. You're looking for a flexible strategic partnership.

Mostly 3's - Your a mid-size to larger agency that has client-facing Account Managers and Strategists already. Your partnership might not encompass most of the client success aspects, but don't let that mean you shouldn't choose an agency with excellent communication skills. You're going to want to find a team that is highly organized and transparent with their communication to prep you for any question your client might have. Team meetings will be a staple in your normal workflow. You're looking for fulfillment only.

Congratulations! Now you know what type of partnership you're looking for. There's another layer to this though and it's going to be one of the most important decisions you make. One that relies heavily on trust and communication.

Chapter Two Reflection

What are my top 5 personal and/or professional reasons to scale now or in the future?

1. _____

2. _____

3. _____

4. _____

5. _____

What are my top 3 important needs in order to scale in the immediate future?

1. _____

2. _____

3. _____

Based on the White Label Partnership Assessment, my ideal partnership is a...

_____

THREE

White Label Partnership Benefits

Now that you know what type of partner you're looking for, let's discuss how to make the most out of that relationship. Benefits can range from simple things like support with your own sales efforts to the ultimate goal which is increasing your agency's recurring revenue and client retention rate.

Benefits of a Full-Service Agency

If you are unsure if a white label full-service marketing agency is for you, there are plenty of benefits worth considering. Here are some of the ones we think are key.

Saves Money

It is a fact. A white label full-service marketing agency, like 51Blocks, helps save you money. Hiring a single full-time expert who provides one or more of the services you can get with a white label marketing agency can cost you quite a bit. From executive pay to overhead, benefits, and more – your company needs to shell out the dough when it comes to professional, high-quality online marketing support. In addition to this, you may not require their particular service all of the time. With a white label full-service marketing agency, however, you can hire an entire team of experts for less it costs to retain your own employee. Additionally, you can save even more money by hiring them only when you need them.

Saves Time

In addition to the money it takes to hire a professional, it also takes time and effort to hunt down the right person for the job. Not only do you need to find an individual who shares your business passion, mindset and goals – you also need to have an in-depth understanding of the services you will need in order to properly evaluate their resume and portfolio. A white label full-service marketing agency, however, has already done the footwork here.

At 51Blocks, we only hire experts who excel in marketing and search engine optimization (SEO) strategies to ensure you get quality support every time you need it. This means you have more time to focus on other aspects of your business.

Expert Service

A white label full-service marketing agency offers a wide range of professional campaign features, such as SEO forecasting, social media management, pay-per-click (PPC) analytics, webpage development, and more. At 51Blocks, we assemble teams to fit your needs. This means you have a team of high-trained, experienced experts at your fingertips anytime you need them. Their quality work, specialized focuses, unique experiences, and integrated approach ensures every potential issues or request is handled quickly and professionally.

Increase Your Portfolio of Expertise

Because of the expert services you received from a quality white label marketing agency, you are also able to expand your own portfolio of expertise. Why? Because, with white label partnerships, your brand is able to take all the credit for the work provided by your partner. A white label partnership means you can resell your partner's services as your own, netting yourself all the accolades their quality work provides.

Scalable Support for Flexible Growth

Coupled with our expert services is the potential for flexible growth. Every business wants to see the positives increase as the negatives decrease. With our scalable packages, you can offer the services best suited to your customers' needs. This means you can support everything, from small startups to huge corporations.

Happy Clients

Because a white label full-service marketing agency is able to enhance your portfolio with their expertise, you can provide a more thorough campaign to your clients. By doing so, you will likely see an increase in customer satisfaction and positive feedback. (Have you seen the average length of our customer relationships at 51Blocks? At 2.5 years, our average customer relationship proves that our white label services encourage loyalty.)

More Business

We all know happy clients tend to help encourage potential new customers to look into your services as well. This means a white label marketing agency does not just save you time and money, it also helps increase your business and net you new clients. Having the time to sell and not fulfill will help you grow at a much faster pace.

White Label Benefits For You

White labeling allows you to expand your service offerings with minimal effort. The agency you partner with will take care of the work while you focus on running your business and developing client relationships.

You don't have to know SEO to use white label services. The agency you partner with will have an experienced and highly skilled staff who understand the best practices and what it takes to improve the client's ROI. They will offer you complete support, so you always have an expert on your side.

Why hire someone in-house when you can partner with an white label agency that already knows and understands the business? This partnership will save you time and money in the long run simply because you don't have to devote time and resources into scouting out talent and investing in a new technical infrastructure.

Knowing how to have every question answered, every strategy explained, and having a team help set the proper expectations will help you under promise and over deliver every time.

By re-selling services to clients, you increase your bottom line. If choose to partner with an agency that offers ongoing monthly subscriptions, your cash flow increase is only limited by the number of customers you get to sign up.

Your end goal is time and financial freedom. Spending more time with your family or doing the things you love and finding a team that can increase your bottom line so you can sleep easy is the goal of your partner as well. They work hard, so you can enjoy the freedom you deserve from the day-to-day.

<u>Chapter Three Reflection</u>

What are the most important benefits for me to want this type of partnership?

_____

_____

_____

_____

How will my clients benefit from my partnership?

_____

_____

_____

_____

FOUR

Preparing for a Partnership

Shopping for a White Label Agency

You've now defined what type of partner you need and the benefits you'll be gaining by scaling through white labeling. Now it's time to shop for the right partner and ensure you have your pricing model established. This will be important information when choosing your partner as not all costs are the same nor is the value you'll get.

In order to assess possible partners, ask the following questions to take a deeper dive into each agency's process.

Questions To Ask Possible Partners

1. What is your competitive advantage working with an agency of my size?
2. What does your onboarding process look like?
3. What does your organizational structure look like?

4. What does your communication process look like?
5. What does your reporting process look like?
6. What deliverables do you provide each month?
7. What is your process of developing a campaign strategy?
8. Who will be owning the campaign?
9. How do you support my agency in the sales process?
10. Is there a minimum number of clients I need to have?
11. Is there a partnership fee involved?
12. What are your agency's core values?

If you can get the sales person to screenshare a little about their own processes, great! If not, be sure to ask for more information like case studies, example deliverables, and partner information that you can help base your final decision on. You might also try meeting more members of their team in a follow up call.

Even if you only plan to start with a test client (or your agency's marketing) -- you'll want to get a feel for their quality of work. A transparent agency will be happy to provide you with anything you ask for.

Establishing Your Pricing Model

What is a healthy profit margin for digital marketing services (Value Issue)? This varies depending on which digital marketing service is being marked up. For example, websites can be marked up 20-150%

since it is difficult to tell the difference between a $3,000 website and an $8,000 website. For SEO, we have found that if services are marked more than 35% there needs to be additional value added. This is because it is often hard to show the value of a large markup in SEO. You don't want your client to consider a cheaper alternative, but you also want to make a profit.

Standard monthly pricing package margins

- Local SEO - 20-25%
- National SEO - 20-25%
- PPC - 20-30%
- Social Ads - 10-15%
- Content - 25-50%
- Website Development - 20-150%
- Hosting - 20-100%
- E-commerce- 20-25%

What happens if your agency and white label charge the same? This is a conversation we've certainly had with our partners before they sign on. If you're charging less than $100/hour (which is what we charge as a direct hourly cost), then you're likely not offering a level of customer service and quality that you 1) could be with the right team and structure or 2) uncomfortable increasing your costs because you don't think your clients are willing to pay that.

Rather than asking a potential partner to reduce their fee, evaluate the value you're gaining by increasing to meet your direct cost with a margin you're happy with. What are clients going to gain in quality, results, and customer service? Is that important to your potential clients? You can be the judge to weigh your options, but in our experience the level of service you raise your agency by paying for a quality partner increases the lifetime value for your business and reputation in the long run.

Custom Quotes vs Package Pricing

It's a common standard in the digital marketing industry to have packages. You bundle several services within one fee for your client each month and they never see the buckets where their spend is allocated. This is certainly a feasible way to sell services and even have your new partner work within what you sell depending on what you're allocating. As long as your profit margin can still justify the results they're getting from the campaign spend overall, there usually isn't an issue.

The only time we have ever seen an issue with package pricing and the value gap has been extreme markups. Clients begin to wonder why they're paying $2000 a month to your agency and the meter for their service is moving slowly. This is when the responsibility lies on you to provide them with additional value (this might be in the form of tools, resources, or consulting -- in addition to the services they're getting).

Custom quotes are the best course of action for clients who may have specific goals (to hit X% increase by X date) or ones who might have special circumstances (bad digital marketing in the past or a new site would be examples).

Custom Quotes

How to create a custom quote for your client

Keep your profit margin in mind, while also keeping in mind the realistic cost of a campaign. You want your client to see the value in what you are offering them. You don't want them to go looking for a cheaper quote, but you also want to cover your direct costs and make a profit.

Our process for determining direct cost quotes

Before providing a direct cost quote to you, our team takes a few things into account. Your client's location, competitors, current site health, their user experience and their overall goals are looked over, to create a plan that is unique to your client. This ensures that all their needs are met and they can see the most benefit from their plan.

Business details required for a custom quote

- Client's overall marketing activities
- Previous SEO/PPC/Social
- Client's budget (if applicable)
- Client's goals
- Client's location and ideal targeted locations
- Client's competitors
- Keywords that the client would like to rank for

This information is necessary to tailor a custom fitted plan to your client. As well as, to come up with the realistic cost it will take to deliver what they need.

Do you have a client in mind right now for this? Visit https://mydigitalform.com/white-label-quote/ to get your custom quote for any of our digital marketing services.

Package Pricing

Website - $2,500
Custom Designed Website
Content Developed for 10 Primary Service
Foundational SEO

Ongoing Monthly Fee - $2,250
PPC Management - Adwords & Facebook
Review Automation System
Reputation Management System
Monthly eMail Newsletter

Content Developed for 10 City Pages
On-page website optimization
Claim & Update Online Directory Listings
Monthly Blogging
Ongoing Citation Development
Keyword Tracking & Reporting
Analytics Tracking & Reporting
Phone Tracking & Reporting
Hyper Fast Website Hosting

SEO & PPC

Website - $3,500
Custom Designed Website
Develop content for all service & 10 city pages
Foundational SEO

Ongoing Monthly Fee- $2,750
Lead Capture Guide & Follow up Sequence
On-page website optimization
Conversion Optimization

PPC Management - Adwords & Facebook
Review Automation System
Reputation Management System
Monthly eMail Newsletter
Content Developed for 10 City Pages
On-page website optimization
Claim & Update Online Directory Listings
Monthly Blogging
Ongoing Citation Development
Keyword Tracking & Reporting
Analytics Tracking & Reporting
Phone Tracking & Reporting
Hyper Fast Website Hosting

Online Dominance Complete

A common question we are asked is how we can fit into an agency's existing packages. Simply put, you can determine how much of the budget is put towards any given service and we will set the expectation for how quickly a client can see results.

The most important factor to determine when developing packages is the driving force of value. What is the client paying for? What service in your package will show them the most value? This is where you should focus their spend. If you're targeting a particular niche, developing packages is often easier because you're aware of what your niche's competitive landscape looks like.

Therefore you can break your packages into levels that encompass more or less. Just keep in mind that the conversation will always revolve around the value they will gain from the flat fee they're paying for everything in your package.

51 BLOCKS

QUICK TIPS

The best way to support your white label partner here is to remind clients of the value in other services that may not be managed by your outsourced team. For example, if they're getting tools to self manage their online reviews, keep them engaged by proactively sharing good news about positive reviews or helping them respond to poor reviews. Show them how this has helped their business growth in addition to the lead generation activities.

Chapter Four Reflection

My ideal margin is _____ %

My current package pricing is _____

_____

My current hourly pricing is _____

My direct cost will be _____

My markup will be _____%

My gross profit margin will be _____

Gross profit = potential sales - cost

Markup = gross profit / cost

FIVE

Selling Your Services

So you've decided on what you want to offer and how you're going to price it. Time to get creative with your copy! Pitching the service is a big part of enticing your potential clients to sign on. Adding a landing page for each new service is a good way to showcase your packages and service descriptions. Remember, you don't need to tell them everything. It's an appetizer portion of the meal. Keep it simple and clear.

Sample Service Descriptions

Looking for some inspiration? Here's an overview of how we speak about our services. If you're already selling these services, ensure you're speaking to your competitive advantage or benefits -- not just that you provide a service.

Hosting

Not all hosting services care about their clients, but we do. We cover all of the gray areas, so you don't have to worry. Here is what our hosting service can offer you.

- Backups - We offer 90 days of backups, just in case you ever need them.
- Updates - We go above and beyond to ensure your core, theme and plugins are always up to date. An up to date site is the first defense against hackers.
- Performance - We ensure your website is also running at peak performance. Fast loading pages are valuable to SEO success.
- Security - We give you SSL (secure certificate), most places would charge you $50-$100 for this. SSL helps with SEO and is one of the things that Google looks for when crawling sites.
- Uptime Monitoring - We monitor your site and check it for uptime every 5 minutes. This ensures your site is never down and you're never missing out on traffic. We currently host over 350 WordPress websites successfully, with no down time to date.

Website Design

It isn't just about how a search engine views your client's site. It is also important for site visitors to enjoy their experience. Ease of use and clarity plays a big role in how many people choose to stay and use your site. These are the things we address.

- Ease of Use -How easy can visitors find what they are looking for?

- Accessibility - Is the site mobile friendly? It is important that mobile users can easily navigate your site, not just view it. Accessibility also takes into account devices that are used by vision, or hearing impaired visitors.
- SEO - Some website features benefit SEO and other hurt it. Things like in site search engines, blogs and shopping carts can hurt SEO if not set up properly.
- Security - Whenever information from site visitors is collected, you have to be sure to keep that information protected. The site needs to be secure from hackers, malware and other dangers, we take this into consideration.

SEO

SEO is a key factor in every website's success, a website will never get anywhere if no one ever sees it. Here's what your client can expect from our SEO services.

- Thorough Investigation - We start off every SEO project with a keyword analysis, competition investigation, a site analysis and a business consultation. We lay it out so your client can see where they are and what it's going to take to get where they want to be. We are always realistic with time frames and the investment it will take to see a return on their investment.
- Strategy - We create a detailed plan that outlines our strategy and covers exactly

what we will be doing to get your client results.

- Consultations - We stay in communication with your client, so they know exactly what they're achieving.
- Personalized Service - We strive to put ourselves in your client's place and understand their business, so we can drive traffic to their site that will be beneficial to them.

PPC

A successful campaign is always the goal when venturing into PPC and we strive to make that success happen. Here's what our PPC services can offer your client.

- Experience and Dedication
- Communication
- Detailed Keyword Analysis
- PPC Bid Management and Campaign Analysis

Content

The information on a site plays a big role in how people perceive it and how likely they are to continue using it. When a potential customer visits your client's site the content they see is their first impression and we help make first impressions good ones. Our content service ensures relevant, researched and up to date content.

- We will work to reach key influencers, build relationships through social media, and create content that may go viral.
- Most importantly we will represent your brand in the best possible light!

Questions to Ask Prospects

Once you begin having sales calls, it's going to be important for your partner to have as much information as possible. This can be helpful if you're preparing to ask a partner for a custom quote or just getting enough understanding of the need to choose the right package for your client.

51 BLOCKS

QUICK TIPS Keep track of your sales intake information and notes to share with your team so they can onboard more efficiently and have a smooth tie over from sales. This will help all teams maintain the expectations set in the sales process along with developing deeper onboarding questions.

Getting your prospect on the path to saying "Yes" and making the initial sale can be difficult, but it doesn't have to be. Here are some questions you can ask yourself, the answers will in turn help you close the deal. You don't know what to offer them, if you don't know what they need.

Tips For Selling Digital Marketing Packages

- Understand how your client makes money -
  What is their sales process and how can
  you improve it?

- Get as much detail about the business as
  possible - What is their goal, their main
  customer base, who are their competitors
  and how can you give them a 'one up'?

- Understand the client's goals - What is it
  that they are trying to achieve and how can
  you help them climb that mountain faster?
  What is their idea of success?

- Set reasonable expectations for KPIs -
  Don't over sell what you can do for them.
  What is a reasonable expectation for them?

- Previous/Current Marketing Efforts -
  Emphasize the 51B holistic approach. Don't
  tell them what they're doing wrong, just
  emphasize how you can enhance their

current efforts and bring new tools to the table.

- Budget - What is their budget? Keep services realistic to what they can afford, don't try to sell them a yacht if they can only pay for a sailboat.

- Communication Expectations - What kind of communication do they expect to receive and how can you meet those expectations?

- Understanding the Competitive Landscape - Do they understand what they are up against? Do they have big name competitors and how can you help level the playing field?

- Take a Digital Marketing course to enhance your skills of selling. We generally say you can't sell a car if you only know how to ride a bike. Digital Marketer has some great courses across every service you can sign up and access - https://www.digitalmarketer.com/

Warm/Hot Leads

If you're an established agency, you likely already have a hot lead sales and follow up process. If it's working, you can skip this section and do your thing!

For the new agency owner, here are some of our tips for what to do with those who are quick to move on your services.

Warm and hot leads are people who know about you and know about your services, but haven't yet chosen to purchase these services from you, even if they're thinking about it. There are few pieces of information to get from them that can help sway them to a sale.

More information about their business - You'll be better equipped to connect with a lead if you can relate with them and in order to do this you need to know what they do.

More information about what they need - Client's don't want to invest in things that don't benefit them, in order to land a sale you need to know what you can give them, that they don't already have.

More information about what tools they're already implementing - If you know what they're already doing, you have enough information to convince them that you can help do it better.

Maximizing Upsell Opportunities

Upselling to offer your new service, or even a current one you're utilizing a new partner for can take form in many ways. Often times the most appropriate course is to either sell your existing clients on your new offering or with the help of your new partner identify upsells to an existing campaign.

Upselling is a strategy in every market, it not only benefits the buyer, but also the seller. The main thing we keep in mind when trying to upsell is figuring out what package B can offer, that package A doesn't and why that extra bit is important to your client. We won't sell them something they don't need.

- Making sure there is an adequate foundation for digital marketing - This all starts with a great website. Many times your clients might want SEO or PPC, but without a conversion oriented site, they will see little value from these services. Websites are one of the most common upsells initially.
- Aligning upsells with client goals - Upsells are based on a client request or an area of opportunity. We only upsell clients when ROI justifies the campaign adjustment
- Utilizing your partner to develop pitches - We are very experienced in researching the value in different markets for clients. Let us know what service you would like to expand

or we can do a full audit of opportunities for clients.

How to upsell organically

- Understanding the right time to upsell - The best time to upsell is when the current budget won't allow you to meet the client's goals, or if there are areas of opportunity that the client isn't effectively pursuing.
- Basing upsells on success (how can we do even better?) - Scaling is a huge part of marketing and once something starts working and showing results, it's only logical to apply the strategy to as many areas of the campaign as possible.
- Showcase your victories to expand the strategy - Capitalize on the gains made with your client's current strategy by offering campaign enhancements. Are they only getting one blog a month that sees a lot of traffic? Then they should consider expanding their budget to accommodate more of that content.

Chapter 5 Reflection

Do I have these resources in place to sell digital marketing? What needs to be provided by my partner?

Me	My Partner	Resource
☐	☐	Offer or Package Scope
☐	☐	Case Studies
☐	☐	Dedicated landing pages
☐	☐	Example deliverables
☐	☐	Proposal Templates
☐	☐	Reporting Examples
☐	☐	Lead Magnets

My needs to begin selling are...

_____

_____

SIX

Partnership Workflow

Get your client to sign on the dotted line? Hooray! You're ready to roll into onboarding. Depending on the agency you've chosen to partner with, they may have their own process for proposals and invoicing.

Ours consists of a simple agreement, invoice, and scheduling the onboarding call. All of which can be done in about 2 business days. Here's a little glimpse at the 51Blocks process for signing on your clients.

Step 1	Step 2	Step 3
PARTNERSHIP PROPOSAL SIGNED	INVOICE FOR DIRECT FEE (PAID)	ONBOARDING CALL SCHEDULED

It's really that simple. Each one of our agreements can also include special customization for language you may also use in your own proposals (which you'll be using to sign the client). A good partner will ensure every detail you need to feel comfortable with the scope is in the proposal.

Fee Schedule

This is an area where white labeling can get complicated if you and your partner don't have proper expectations set with each other. You're now dealing with a direct cost to a provider and the client's billing. Most partners will be collecting their fees up front, like 51Blocks, which means you're going to want to ensure you either collect payment from your client before the onboarding call or you have enough to cover while you're waiting on their payment. If you're an agency that follows a Net30 model, you'll want to speak with your partner and see how you can work together on invoicing dates that will make sense.

Remember, this is covering the cost of an entire team's overhead to work on your client's campaign.

51 BLOCKS

In order to never see a delay in your client's services, you should always keep track of your invoicing dates and ask your partner to keep auto-pay active. Most partners will require some type of 30-day notice so you'll know when to alert the team to end the auto-pay and run your final invoice should your client choose not to continue.

Onboarding

Onboarding a new or existing client is paramount in setting the right impression. As we all know, first impressions mean everything when setting the tone for trust and rapport. The onboarding process should be smooth and effective. Your team is going to need to know some basic details. In addition to the finer details for the kickoff. These are all things that you can provide if this is an existing client or our a white label team can gather after the onboarding call.

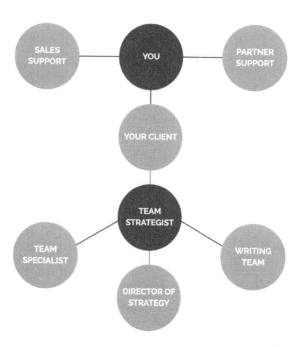

Below are examples of what those requirements might be.

- Google access for our team
- Access to an email for communication with the client
- Access to any 3rd-party tracking/sales tools
- Provide branding materials, logos and any other assets needed to represent your business
- Access to previous marketing reports
- Website access for our team

Onboarding Questions

There are several ways an onboarding call might be handled to kick things off. If you're utilizing a full service team, the Operations Manager or Director of Strategy will likely be leading the call along with the Strategist assigned to the campaign. This is a chance for your client to see the entire team and it's meant to be a high energy call ensuring your client walks away with clarity and concrete expectations.

If you're remaining point of contact for your white label team, you'll want to gather all of the information for your team before the call. Keep in mind, on most calls the team will ask questions as they arise organically from the conversation so it's best to have a follow up call with the team to ensure they're all set before asking them to proceed.

Here are some of our own onboarding questions we ask to give the team a nice baseline of information.

Business Overview

1. Please introduce our team to your brand and the audience we'll be targeting in our digital marketing campaign.

2. Is there anywhere outside of your listed business address we should be aware of to target or avoid?

3. Talk to us about your competitors. Can you name the top 3-5 and tell us why you have determined them to be your competition in the market and what makes you different?

4. Apart from lead generation, rankings, and increased site engagement are there any other goals you have in mind for this campaign which will define it as successful for you?

General Marketing

1. What other marketing activities outside of SEO & PPC are you currently doing and how well does each effort perform for ROI?

2. What marketing efforts can be improved?

3. What does your sales process look like? Can you take us through the steps of how you qualify a lead?

4. Talk to us about your most profitable services. Do you have any that are bigger ticket items for you in terms of profit?

5. Do you know what the average sale amount is overall for your business? Does it depend on the service?

6. What is the lifetime value of a sale? Do you have more one-time or returning customers?

7. What would you say the average close rate is for your team?

SEO

1. Have you had previous SEO work done on the site and how long ago was that?

   a. Did they provide you with any reporting that we can reference for their work?

2. Content is an important aspect of SEO since it will increase the number of pages indexed and allow Google to match you with more search terms. What is your current workflow for blog/content production on the site?

3. Are you comfortable with us writing for you or optimizing content you write?

4. What are topics you would like us to discuss and ones we should stay away from?

5. What are the needs that people have when they use you for a solution?
   a. Are there any search terms you think they type in specifically?

6. Have you engaged in any previous paid backlinking activity?

7. How well would you say the site currently engages visitors?

8. What is the way people tend to convert (form or phone call) and how are you tracking the organic form submissions or phone calls in your sales process?

9. Are there any specific search phrases you type in yourself to check on your SEO health?

PPC

1. What does Adwords look like for us stepping in now? Are campaigns live, paused, or non-existent?

2. Have you ever engaged in call-only or display ads?

3. Have you already determined the URLs of the landing pages to use in the campaigns or will you need us to build out new landing pages?

4. What is the primary action you would like people to take with your Adwords campaign?

5. Do you have any offers that we're able to use in the ad copy?

6. What should we stay away from when writing ad copy? Is there anything that you think might draw in the wrong type of lead?

7. Have you previously used or currently use a different phone number for ads from CallRail or any other call tracking software?

Social

1. What are your current social media efforts?

2. What are your goals for your social media campaign?

3. Do you have any high quality or photos we can use for the campaign?

4. Do you have Facebook for Business setup for your page?

5. Are you using any landing pages?

6. Are you comfortable with us writing ad copy and sending it to you for approval? Is there any copy that we should not use?

7. Who is your ideal client/customer? (Interests, hobbies, what they read, what resources they use, thought leaders in your space)

51 BLOCKS

QUICK TIPS

Ensure your partner has a solid follow up process. 51Blocks for example has a 7 touch onboarding process which consists of plenty of information to ensure your client feels they're on the same page with our team each step of the way while we're in the strategic planning phase. Be sure to ask your partner what the follow up process is and ask how you can work together to overcome stalls if a client becomes unresponsive.

Communication & Management Workflow

Understanding how your partner will manage your client is a discussion you'll generally have when you're in the discovery process shopping for the right partner, but this can vary.

At 51Blocks, this varies for us by partner and even by client from each partner. Some clients need more hand holding, some are extremely busy and want one call a month, and others like a blend of education and data throughout the month. Something we provide partners which has been very successful is a shared inbox. All emails from any of your clients can be sent to one email address under your domain name. This is one central location for all of your clients to email in and utilize the entire team.

Our system allows an internal team member to quickly acknowledge your client and assign to the right person. Not only does this allow you to have the transparency (should you want it) into every email our team is sending out, but it allows our management team to proactively help with any elevated tones or issues before they become fires.

Deliverables

Your white label partner should be providing all client facing deliverables in a format that incorporates your branding. Get to know what deliverables your white label partner provides in their own workflow and see if they're also comfortable working with yours.

Examples of branded deliverables:
- 90-day roadmaps
- Keyword research
- Writing samples
- Monthly reporting

The most important thing is to be consistent. Establishing a unique workflow for your clients outside of what the white label provides should be perfectly acceptable, but apply it across the board so they can train team members in a uniform process as you scale and they bring on more strategists to your accounts.

Reporting

For years our agency tried to find better ways to show value through monthly reporting. Let's be honest, most clients aren't reading those generic data reports you're sending because they're either too hard for the client to digest or they're uninterested in the technical information. Our agency was determined to solve this and come up with a better solution to keep retention high and clients engaged with the impact their campaigns were having on their bottom line.

In 2018, our CEO, set off to build one robust reporting system that could contain it all. The data our team needed to make decisions, the information that could tell a story year-over-year, and the visuals clients needed to show how we impacted their bottom line. In the summer of 2019, aDash was unveiled. Suddenly we went from being an agency with standard monthly reporting, to a partner who can show a client how each marketing dollar translates into LTV, ROAS, and sales for their business.

We're often asked why we branded it outside of 51Blocks and the truth is, it's powerful enough to be a stand alone solution for all agencies. Our partners can utilize this as their own, even if we aren't actively working on all or any campaigns.

Here's everything we showcase in our monthly reporting:

1. Overview of monthly campaign spend, sales, and ROI
2. Google Analytics KPIs (total traffic, engagement, etc)
3. YOY total traffic and organic charts
4. Medium performance

5. Source performance
6. Landing page performance
7. Google My Business actions
8. Google My Business YOY performance
9. Keyword movement
10. Citation building
11. Google Search Console clicks, impressions, and CTR
12. GSC top queries
13. GSC top pages
14. MOM tasks
15. ROI
16. LTV
17. ROAS
18. CPC

Calculating ROI is simple and easy to explain to your client.. Simply divide your campaign budget by the number of leads you have in the month or year. We can help you take this a step further by tracking:

- LTV of a client - How many times customers or clients return to the business for products and services per year. Knowing these stats allows you to create a strategy that maximizes profit from your leads
- Close rate - This is the percentage of leads that turn into sales. Leveraging this stat will help you get better leads and optimize your strategy for more conversions.
- Top converting pages/paths - These are the pages a user visited that led to a conversion. Keeping track of converting pages will help you get more from your

content strategy. This will also show you what pages you need to improve and will identify the parts of your website that are difficult to navigate.

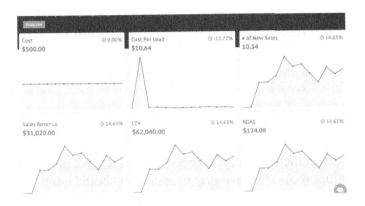

Want to learn more about our unique reporting tool that showcases a client's success? Visit www.adash.io and check out our demo!

SEVEN

Managing Your Partnership

Being a good white label partner

Partnerships are relationships. At its core, it's based around trust, mutual respect, and communication. Your role in the partnership is to support and remove any roadblocks should it be hindering the client's success. If you're with a full service agency, it's unlikely you'll be pulled in to much of the conversation as you'll have a management team responsible for this step, but depending on your desire to be involved, you may step in at times to help.

There are a few things you can keep in mind to make sure you are being a good label partner. In any business relationship it is important for there to be no lapse in communication or synchronization. In order to achieve the most, with the least problems we all need to work together. Here are some things we suggest.

Prep our team - It is just as important for you to keep us informed as it is for us to keep you and your client informed. Communication is an important part of any business relationship. Giving us the most information to begin with will set us all up for success. It allows your new team to maintain the expectations you've set with your client and set any new timelines or expectations based on their overall goals.

Understanding and reporting your client's revenue structure

Lifetime Value - What is the total average revenue generated by a customer or patient throughout their engagement with your client's business?

Average Sale - What is the average revenue generated by a single sale to a customer by your client's business?

Current cost per conversion - How many marketing dollars are currently being spent to turn a user into a lead across all channels? This helps establish and show value to your clients. We can apply an industry average as a general measurement if these numbers aren't available.

Close Rate - How many of your leads turn into actual customers?

Fulfillment - Are we a key part of your agencies overall strategy?

Client Management - Communication is the most important part of client management. We rely on a shared inbox for clients so that requests and questions are answered promptly. We also send updates after tasks are completed- no more wondering what your SEO/PPC expert is doing!

Providing monthly reports and meetings on those reports helps us keep the client informed of the value they are receiving from the campaign and it and makes sure that the strategy is always aligned with their goals.

We are also fully equipped to work within your project management tool of choice (e.g. Basecamp, Podio, Asana etc.). We focus on having full transparency, even at the task level, so that we can keep clients informed and work towards the goals of the account.

Defining KPIs together

Most agencies are going to have their own ideals around what should be tracked. Common KPIs around traffic and leads will usually look the same across partners. It's important that you and your partner are on the same page before you go into the campaign.

Defining your client's KPIs can help us to better help your client. Our philosophy of Marketing by

Math is a proprietary, data-driven solution to help your clients increase their revenue. Understanding the relationship between every dollar spent vs every dollar made will not only help to inform our general strategy, but can easily be aligned with your clients' ever-changing goals and ultimately help grow their businesses.

Key performance indicators are the stats that you decide are most important to your business. As such, you will want to pick the stats that impact growth or revenue so that you aren't working on increasing numbers that will do little for your bottom line. This should be a measurable stat so you can gauge the success of your marketing efforts. Some KPIs we recommend tracking are:

- Conversions
- Leads
- LTV of a client and your close rate

51 BLOCKS Establish the campaign KPIs in the sales process. Ask your client what will determine the campaign's success to them and then pass this vital information on before onboarding so your team can kickoff with the right tracking in place. You should get granular with this -- especially if it's around specific keywords.

Checking In

It's perfectly fine if all you want to do is sell. In fact, many of our partners want to solely sell as a way to free up their time. This doesn't mean that you should forget about your clients all together.

Make time to check on your clients once a quarter or ask to be CC'd on their reporting so you can keep up on how things are going.

Happy clients are loyal clients. Here are some things to keep in mind when checking in with your client.

- Satisfaction Level - Are they happy, what could we do to improve their satisfaction?

- Do they understand the reporting data? Being able to understand the data is vital to their understanding of how we are helping and they are benefiting.

- Do they understand the strategy? If they don't understand the strategy they may not grasp the importance of how it will benefit them, and they may do things to undermine it, without knowing.

Discussing the value of work

Not every client can see the value in digital marketing when they have limited visibility to the tasks taking place each month. By offering transparency into the process, you can show value for the services they are receiving.

Through education and open lines of communication, your client will be able to see the effort put forward from their campaign spend and the ROI each month. Always focus on growth, but don't shy away from struggles. Presenting both negative and positive issues on a client's account, we have an opportunity to improve their strategy. You may want to join the monthly reporting calls each month to take part in this discussion.

EIGHT

White Label SEO

SEO is one of the most common services to outsource. Why? If you sell websites, this is an easy add on. If you sell paid media, this is your golden ticket to longer client engagement. SEO is an investment long-term for most clients. On average they will need to understand the expectation is about 6-8 months before seeing a solid ROI, but they will certainly see traffic, ranking, and conversion gains along the way.

Defining the campaign

Every year Google and other search engines get smarter and smarter, which means for marketers defining goals, strategy, and expectations continues to get more and more granular.

It's important to know the cornerstones of your partner's approach to SEO. For example, 51Blocks does not build links. You're probably wondering why since Google tells us it's one of the foundational pieces of the algorithm (which is true).

For most small businesses, every single dollar counts. As an hourly agency, we've never seen that putting the hour or two per month in link outreach trumps putting that extra few hours towards conversion rate optimization, technical/local SEO, or content. We understand links are important -- we just choose a strategy which allows us to directly track and report on the efforts that directly impact conversions.

51Blocks Approach to SEO

SEO isn't a one-size-fits-all approach for our team. We're invested in the client's business and create holistic custom strategies around everything else they might be working on. Our approach has been proven to drive 20-30% more conversions YOY. Here are some of the pillars of our campaigns.

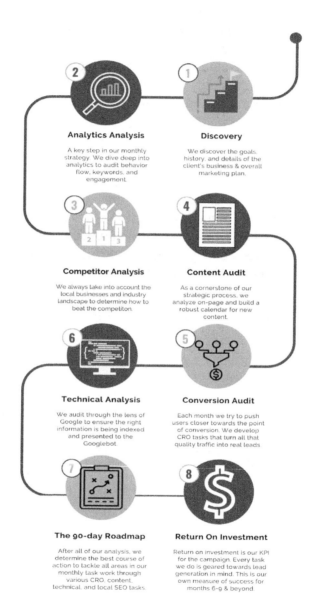

Content

Content is a cornerstone of our campaigns. It's not just developed to rank, it's strategically created to convert. We like to educate our clients around what topics are information vs solution-oriented so they understand exactly what we're going after for searchability. This is especially important for service based clients who have consumers who like to shop around before making an attempt to contact. Dentists and lawyers are a great example of clients who succeed with solution based information which showcases a touch of thought leadership along with the voice and tone of their brand.

It's not just about new copy either. While location pages and new service pages are great for foundational SEO, copy updates and optimization are key to taking an ok site and turning it into a traffic machine. Simply put, the more quality authentic information we give Google to digest, the more likely we'll see strong improvements over the campaign.

Thought leadership, long for content, lead gen magnets, and eBooks are also great forms of content we believe in producing as needed for a client too. These might be used for pop-ups on the website or offers across paid campaigns to assist with increased conversions.

Conversion Rate Optimization

Another cornerstone of our campaign strategy is CRO. Traffic from all of that great indexable content is great, but what do you do with it once it's on the site? Conversion rate optimization can take place in many forms. We like to begin by analyzing where we're losing the most traffic and place design and copy edits on page to see if we can increase both engagement and bounce rate. We also like to understand the behavior flow and see if we can capture more traffic to move deeper down the funnel.

It all starts with brand awareness and appetizer portions of information on the homepage then layers of information found on interior pages. We get a little nerdy around here with data and like to also test form placement, calls to action, button placement, and several other little details that might help capture and entice someone to contact a business.

Citation Building

Citation building is an element of our local SEO campaigns that are a form of link building. Though not the same as link outreach in a traditional sense, we place a client's information (NAP) on various directories and submit to large aggregators to be pushed out to the most popular online directories. A competitive analysis also tells us which directories we should manually submit to. Our main goal with

citation building isn't to have the most citations --
it's the have the ones that matter and have them as
optimized as possible.

Technical SEO

Schema markup, titles & meta descriptions, and
search console sweeps are just some of the things
we take care of on a technical SEO level. To our
clients we explain this as information and work for
Google vs the user (like CRO). This is where a lot
more of our heavy education comes in for clients.
Because often times they can't see the technical
work we do, they might not see the value. So we
like to inform them about what we're doing, why
we're doing it, and what our goals are.

Setting up your workflow

SEO can be collaborative or your partner can run
the show. This is one service that looks different for
us from one partner to the next. Your workflow
should be setup to help with your goals.

If you're hoping to free up your time, then let your
partner handle all of the communication and setup
processes that will allow you to check in on work
when you want, but not so bogged down with
information it's distracting.

When you're establishing campaign workflows, just
remember to ask yourself:
  1. Is this efficient?
  2. Is this effective?

3. Does this benefit my team and client?

You don't want to create rules for your partner unless you can answer yes to all three questions above.

Tracking

Tracking is essential. This is the only way you're going to show your client how much you've improved their bottom line. Have your team or client confirm that tracking is or will be established before steps are executed against the strategy.

We always like to start with a baseline review in aDash. Once we have access to the basics (analytics, etc) we like to make sure clients understand where our work begins and any trends they might be moving towards in their seasonality. You can also review these benchmark data points quarterly to ensure your YOY progress is on track.

Rebuilding a site without losing rankings

While we take care of CRO in our SEO campaigns, we're not talking a full redesign. Here is a little advice on how you can rebuild a client's site without losing their rankings.

Step One: Establish Your Current Ranking

Whether your site does well or not, determining your current rank is important. After all, some people work hard to establish their current search engine optimization (SEO) rank. Some, however, get lucky and stumble on it! Google Analytics is a great tool to start with if you want to do this yourself. This tool will point out which keywords are bringing in website traffic for you.

Establishing your current rank does two things. It tells you what your most important keywords are. Perhaps more important, it tells you whether you rank is worth the work it takes to save it. After all, if you rank poorly, it might be better to just start from scratch.

Step Two: Establish Your Link Structure and Meta Descriptions

If you are new to SEO and rankings, "link structure" and "meta descriptions" may sound like a foreign language. (The experts at 51 Blocks may understand these phrases now, but like you, we were once new to this as well.) To help make this task easier, it helps to start with a spreadsheet.

Organization Is Key

Determine the current overall structure of your website. List each page of your website down one column of your spreadsheet. This should include

Home, About, Services, and any other pages your site currently maps to.

Retain Relevant Content

This section applies to high-ranking content. It stands to reason that if you are already ranking number one for a specific keyword on one of your pages, leaving the content as it is important. Any changes stand a chance of reducing your ranking at this point.

Preserve the Web Design Architecture

Site architecture should be preserved where possible. Why? Maintaining this structure is your best chance to retain your ranking. This includes both your top-level site hierarchy and linking structure. In most cases, you can make dramatic design updates while leaving the site architecture alone. (Need help accomplishing this? Hiring a white label partner like 51 Blocks can ensure your webpage keeps its ranking while we incorporate your design updates.)

Redirect Where Needed

Remember that spreadsheet we started with? In the rows stemming from each page, you should create a list of links. When your content interlinks to itself, it is important to maintain these links. If any of your URLs have changed, you will need to update the links from your other pages. (If you use WordPress, the Redirection plugin can help you easily identify and replace these links!)

Maintain Meta Descriptions

Have you ever noticed blue titles on websites? The ones with little descriptions under them? These are referred to as "meta descriptions". Webmasters should be able to locate these descriptions on each of your webpages. (If you fail to define them yourself, Google does it for you based on your content.) Whether you identified your meta descriptions or Google did, if you rank well, you want to keep them.

Step Three: Add Google Tools

Often, experts recommend you add two very important Google tools before you transfer your site. Google Analytics and Google Webmaster Tools can help ensure you do not lose any of your current data. They also help ensure your website is properly indexed.

Step Four: Monitor

It is important to always remember that SEO is constantly evolving. This means that you should continue to monitor your site for SEO ranking. For the first several weeks, you will want to monitor your site to ensure you do not lose your current SEO ranking. However, continually researching SEO and keywords can help your site ranking grow.

Things to Avoid

Most websites are not constructed live. They are built on a "staging site". This site helps the developer create the content without live streaming it. (This helps preserve your ranking too! Do not develop your site on a live webpage if you want to preserve your SEO ranking!) In WordPress, you want to make sure you uncheck the "discourage search engines from indexing this site" button. WordPress adds this feature to prevent your staging site from accidental release.

Regardless of your host, you will want to thoroughly check your site once you go live. This includes checking every link on each page. Redirects should take you to the new associated webpage. Reviewing these links will help you catch any stray 404 errors early.

Conversions

This is a pretty self explanatory element of SEO, but what are we tracking? Here are some basics on what that might be.
1. Phone calls
2. Form fills
3. Downloads
4. Subscribers
5. eCommerce purchases

Example 90-day roadmap

Objective: Our goal is to increase your search visibility and organic traffic to the site over the next 90 days. By targeting the right keywords, maintaining site health, and building authoritative content for the site, we will establish them as a trusted leader in your industry. Keep in mind that SEO is a long-term investment which allows you to own your place on the first page, rather than renting like Pay-Per-Click. Generally, months 6-9 show the most growth from the baseline point. This strategy is never set in stone and each month the forecast is re-evaluated to include any pressing or urgent items that need to be completed.

Month 1
Establishing Your Foundation & Tools for Success
- Analyze current site content for quality & areas of opportunity
- Establish SEO keyword list with keyword research & client insights
- Optimize all main level navigation title tags & meta descriptions which tell Google where to send your organic visitors (keyword mapping)
- Add SEO keyword list in ranking software to track positive & negative movement
- Establish Google Analytics & Google Search Console to obtain site data for baseline reporting

- Create Google My Business profile for all US locations
- Establish KPIs in Google Analytics for custom dashboard views
- Backlink Evaluation
- Moz directory submission
- Baseline Reporting

Month 2
Analyzing Data & Implementing On-site & Off-site SEO Strategy
- Monthly Reporting
- Monthly Citation Audit
- Optimize Google My Business Profile
- Citation Build for Google My Business visibility
- Content Calendar & Onsite Evaluation
- Optimize Authoritative Blog Content
- Internal Linking
- Internal Page Titles & Metas
- Add Optimized Sitemap to Google Search Console
- Ongoing Crawl Error Evaluation & Redirects
- Create 2-3 pieces of content

Month 3
Analyzing KPI Progress & Continue Foundational SEO Strategy
- Standard Monthly Reporting
- Monthly Citation Audit
- Citation Build for Google My Business visibility
- Content Additions (based on strategy)

- Internal Linking
- Service Page Audits
- Ongoing Crawl Error Evaluation & Redirects
- Site Speed Evaluation & Optimization (as needed)
- Additional Keyword Research
- Create 2-3 pieces of content
- New 90-day plan

NINE

White Label PPC

Paid search is a quick way to get your client leads when they need it faster than a solution like SEO. Our team can do everything from research, create ad copy, and setup the new campaigns along with monthly optimization. A good partner is not going to treat PPC like a set it and forget it service, it will get weekly attention and continuous tweaking to get the lowest CPA and highest conversions for your client's business.

Calculating PPC ROI

The amount spent to acquire a sale or a lead. You can calculate cost per conversion at any time by dividing the total amount spent by the number of leads.

Total Cost of Campaign/Number of Leads = Cost Per Conversion

Return on Ad Spend (ROAS)

ROAS is the metric used to determine the value and outcome of an advertising campaign. ROAS helps calculate the return on every dollar spent and how much revenue was earned. The higher a campaign's ROAS, the higher return with the bare minimum being set at a break even point so that the client doesn't lose money. You can calculate ROAS by dividing the profit from the ad campaign by the cost of the ad campaign.

Profit From Ad Campaign/Cost of Ad Campaign = ROAS

We can help you take these metrics a step further by tracking:

LTV of a client - How many times customers or clients return to the business for products and services per year. Knowing these stats allows you to create a strategy that maximizes profit from your leads

Close rate - This is the percentage of leads that turn into sales. Leveraging this stat will help you get better leads and optimize your strategy for more conversions.

Cost/Conversion Target versus Cost Per Acquisition (CPA) - This is the target cost you'd like to acquire a lead or sale for versus the cost-per-conversion that is achieved on the actual campaign.

Crucial PPC KPIs

Clicks

Clicks and impressions are probably the singularly most important basic metrics that any account manager should be watching on their PPC campaigns. Clicks refer to simply the number of times an ad was clicked on in a campaign.

Impressions

The second basic PPC metrics to watch is impressions. Impressions refer to the number of times an advertisement is displayed.

Cost Per Click

The average amount that you pay for an ad is called the cost per click. This figure can vary wildly from industry to industry and can be higher for some keywords depending on the competition in the market. You can often bring down your cost per click by utilizing longtail keywords, but if you want to remain competitive for your core competency, this may be ill-advised.

Click Through Rate (CTR)

You can easily decipher the CTR of your campaigns by dividing the number of clicks by the number of impressions.

# of Clicks / # of Impressions = CTR

Impression Share

Impression share measures the number of impressions your campaign receives versus the number of impressions it could have received. If the total number of searches performed for the targeted keyword was 1,000 but your ad only appeared 800 times out of those searches you have an 80% impression share and 20% lost impression share.

Looking at the lost impression share gives you the data you need to decide whether to increase your ad spend budget or raise bids. Lost impression share metrics allow you to find out how many impressions were lost due to budget constraints or low ad rank due to poor quality scores or bids.

 You can calculate the clicks and conversions you could have received if you had not lost those impressions by the equation below:

# of Searches Performed for Keyword / # of Times Your Ad Was Shown = Impression Share

Conversion Rate

Conversion rate is the rate at which people convert. In some cases, this can mean a form fill, others a phone call. In its simplest form, it's the number of people who buy. Conversion rate measures how often clicks are made on your campaigns result in a conversion action- a sale, lead, sign-up, etc. You can calculate your conversion rate by utilizing the following equation:

# of People Who Took Action / # of People Who Clicked On Campaign = Conversion Rate

Should you sell PPC?

To figure out if PPC is worth it, first you need to figure out what a lead is worth to your client. Find out how many leads you have had contact with and then see how many of those leads have become customers. Next, find out what the average value of each of these customers is. You should also look at the lifetime value (LTV) of a customer if you have historic data.

Here's an example: In a month long campaign, Jim closed 4 of 10 leads he received. The sales were worth $3,500, $500, $2,250, and $75 ($6,325 total). $6,325 divided by 10 leads means that each lead was worth $632.50 to break even.

Mathematically, the formula looks like this:

$V = (R / L)$

In the formula above, let L equal the total number of leads, let R equal the revenue generated from the closed leads, and let V equal the value of each lead.

If we use the information from the Jim example, the PPC formula looks like this:

$632.50 = (6{,}325 / 10)$

Example 90-day roadmap

Objective: Looking forward, our goal is to leverage the data in the account and create a new build that is data-driven and conversion-focused. This roadmap is based on the brief overview of the account and the Quarterly Business Review for Q4.

Month 1
Establishing Your Campaigns & Discovery
- Analyze current campaigns for areas of opportunity
- Perform market research and competitor analysis
- Keyword discovery
- Restructure the account with a focus on segmentation
- Review Search Terms to ensure keyword relevancy
- Split test Ad Copy to establish best performers
- Create roadmap of industry landing pages based on insights and competitive analysis
- Split test landing page design and on-page elements to discover best-performing CTA's
- Establish a strategy for Remarketing
- Error evaluation
- Monthly Presentation
- Baseline Report

Month 2
Analyzing Data & Optimizations
- Review & optimize Ad Copy using split testing data
- Review keyword performance associated with Avg Position
- Optimize budget allocation
- Review and optimize Ad schedule
- Review and optimize based on the Geographic Report
- Test different Portfolio Bid Strategies
- Develop new opportunities from Search Terms report
- Review landing page performance, segmented by device, and suggest improvements
- Continue to test landing pages
- Review and optimize Remarketing ads and placements
- Monthly report
- Monthly presentation

Month 3
Analyzing KPI Progress & Continued Segmentation
- Further campaign segmentation based upon best performing keywords
- Continued landing page development and testing
- Keyword review and management
- Allocate spend to top performing ad groups

- Review performance across campaigns and eliminate any areas potentially leading to wasted ad spend
- Updated research on competitive environment to ensure PPC competitiveness
- Monthly report
- Monthly presentation

TEN

White Label Website Development

Our Custom Development Process

Timeline for completion will vary depending on the size of the website and assets provided, but we aim for a 45-day design to launch projection.

Discovery

The discovery phase of the project starts with the 51Block's Website Questionnaire. This is where we gather information about your business and begin planning for your new website. We will identify your business needs and create a sitemap with our suggestions for laying out your website's content.

- *Our Actions:* Send Website Questionnaire Form, Research Business Requirements, Develop Sitemap Outline of Website Content

- *What We Need From You:* We need the "down low" on your business. We need to know what you do best and how you offer your services. We will also need you to provide us with any information that may be relevant to creating a dynamic, lead-generating website.

We'll also ask for your Domain & Hosting Credentials, Your Preferred Email & Password for WordPress User Accounts, and a List of Other Users that Will Require Accounts

- *Deliverables:* Website Questionnaire Form, Website Content Sitemap

Design

There are A LOT of different look and feel to websites out there. Choosing the right one for your business and your technical skill level can be difficult without the experience of using many different themes. We are here to provide suggestions if needed otherwise providing sample sites that you like the look and feel of is important. a look and feel you like

- Our Actions: Help you out where we can in regards to look and feel
- *What We Need From You:* In the form we will provide include websites you like and why you like them.

Development

We'll setup a database and install the latest version of WordPress, as well as the following recommended plugins. We will also configure WordPress core settings for you, and begin to develop your website starting with installing the theme you selected. Then, we'll get to work making the theme modifications we've agreed upon in the Theme & Design phase of the project.

Our Actions: WordPress Installation, Installation of Recommended Plugins, Configuration of WordPress Core Settings, Theme Install & Configuration

What We Need From You: Your Preferred Email & Password for User Account, List of Other Users that Will Require Accounts

Deliverables: Document Containing WordPress Website Login Credentials & Staging Website URL Information

With a template site, you will get one round of revisions to make changes to the site. After that, if there are more changes you'd like to make, each round of revisions will be billed hourly, at our hourly rate.

Content Upload

After your theme is installed and configured, your website needs content! We will upload the content you provided for up to 10 pages on your website and develop the layout of these pages within the WordPress CMS. Of course, we can add more than 10 pages of content to your website, but additional pages are not included within this statement of work and will be invoiced for separately.

Afterwards, you will have a chance to review each of the 10 pages. You may request 1 round of consolidated requests for revisions to the pages we've developed for you. Once all of your revision requests are received, we will update the content and finish the website development portion of these landing pages.

- *Our Actions:* Add Content for 10 Web Pages, Revise Web Pages as necessary
- *What We Need From You:* Your Feedback on the content that we have placed on the pages, A consolidated list of any requested page revisions
- *Deliverables:* Email informing you that the content has been added and we need your feedback.

QA & Website Approval

After the 10 web pages have been reviewed and approved, we will go through and make sure that everything on the website is working exactly as intended, such as testing links, submitting test form submissions, reviewing all special functionality and addressing any issues that may arise. After our team has performed our round of QA, it is important for you to review our work again too and make sure everything is in good shape for launch. Then we request written approval for us to launch the completed website.

- *Our Actions:* Perform Thorough Quality Assurance Review of Developed Website, Address Any Pertinent QA Issues that Arise
  - Validate HTML Markup
  - Validate CSS Markup
  - Check Responsiveness
  - Test Web Form
  - Update All Plugins
  - Check for Broken Links
- *What We Need From You:* Your Feedback on the Developed Website, Notification of Any Pertinent Issues You Notice During this Phase, Your Written Approval to Launch the Website

Website Launch & Handoff

Once all of the previous project items have been completed, we'll be ready to launch the site and start sending traffic to it! We perform website launches on Wednesdays only. Your website will be launched on the Wednesday following the date of your launch approval. We'll perform the DNS configuration required to make your new website public. We will also begin allowing access to Meta Robots to the website.

By this time, we should have already received from you the domain and hosting credentials required to launch the site. If we have not received these credentials, your website may be put in an "On Hold" status and subject to a $100 re-engagement fee at our discretion.

Once the site is live, we hand over the keys to your new website and you can take it for a spin – it's all yours!

- *Actions:* Launch Website, Ensure Proper DNS Configuration, Allow Access to Meta Robots
- *What We Need From You:* Availability During the Day of Launch
- *Deliverables:* Document Containing WordPress Website Login Credentials

Hosting

Speed doesn't kill - it increases sales!

Don't believe us? Ask Walmart (cloudflare.com, 2019) who found out for every second of increased page speed, they saw a two percent increase in conversions. In a 2018 research conducted by Google, 53% of mobile visitors abandon a site that takes longer than 3 seconds to load (thinkwithgoogle.com, 2018).

 3 seconds doesn't sound like much, but the same research revealed that it took 15 seconds on average for mobile sites to load. That's 12 seconds of additional time you'd be sitting there waiting to fill your virtual shopping cart.

When it comes to page speed or site speed, every second is vital and the faster your website loads, the more likely you're able to keep users engaged and moving towards the conversion point.

Slow-loading websites don't only force your users to abandon your website but it can also get your website on the wrong side of Google's algorithm. In July 2018, Google rolled out a comprehensive update focused on incorporating Pagespeed as a critical ranking factor. The slower your website, the lower it ranks and the lower it ranks, the less effective all your other SEO strategies will be.

Speed is a serious business. MachMetrics published a research report in 2018 which found out most sites have load times anywhere from 8-11 seconds. Well over the 3-second limit. What does that mean? Most of your competitors have slow websites, so by ensuring your website is the fastest you get an edge over them when it comes to attracting and retaining website visitors and gaining higher rankings on search results. We call this the 'speed advantage'.

The first step in making your website fast is understanding where you stand right now, to do that you need to know exactly how your website is performing. Head over to https://gtmetrix.com and enter your website for a comprehensive test. If it's under 3 seconds and has 90+ page speed and YSlow scores, well done. If not, you're right there with the 9 out of 10 people I ask to do this same thing and they come back with an underwhelming score.

I've tried a lot of different tactics myself to increase speed and you can certainly try to follow some of the standard speed optimization tasks laid out on the GTmetrix, but the best solution we offer is our hyper fast optimized wordpress stack.

The key to outperforming your competitors when it comes to speed, is something called hyper-optimization. This is essentially a custom approach to hosting which runs like the Roadrunner from Looney Tunes on steroids. Their goal is to give every site they touch the 'speed advantage' we mentioned above by using the latest in technology to ensure your website loads and performs at near-instant speeds.

Hosting with 51Blocks also Includes:
- Backups - We offer 90 days of backups
- Updates - We will keep your core, theme, and plugins up to date. This is important just to keep your site from getting hacked.
- Performance - We will make sure your site is loading quickly for SEO purposes
- Security - We give you SSL (secure certificate - most places will charge you $50-$100 for this). This will help with SEO as well and is actually one of the things Google wants to see on sites
- Uptime Monitoring - We will monitor your site for uptime every 5 minutes to make sure your site is never down.

Find out more about our hosting plans at https://www.51blocks.com/pricing/hosting/

ELEVEN

Partnership Success at 51Blocks

About Us

Midwestern Roots, Full Transparency, Proven Results.

51Blocks was started by our very own Michael Borgelt back in 2009 when he was living in Portland, Oregon. As with most startups, he was operating out of his home with a single client in his stable. Initially, the company was a way to supplement his income while Michael pursued his passion of officiating basketball.

Eventually, Michael realized that his true passion was in helping businesses grow and he put all of his efforts into 51Blocks. Shortly after this decision, he hired his first contractor and that's where things really took off.

Integrity and transparency are hard to come by these days. That's why we're completely transparent with our work and don't require contracts. When we agree to work with someone, our singular goal is to help grow their business. This is where Michael's Minnesota roots really start to shine through.

We want people to *want* to work with us, which is why the only "contract" you'll ever have with 51Blocks is a handshake. Off the bat, we provide our new clients with a 90-day roadmap to show exactly what we'll be doing to help their business over the next few months. We provide detailed monthly reporting complete with analytics, task lists, and insights so you know exactly where each of your marketing dollars is going.

Our Mission

1. SET REALISTIC EXPECTATIONS

In our industry, there are people that will claim to give you 1st page rankings overnight. We do not do that. SEO is a long term game. This is why their length of engagement with clients is only 4-6 months. Ours is over 2.5 years. Do we see great rankings, traffic, leads and sales increase— YES! But we are never going to promise that. We begin by performing a rigorous audit of your market space. Who is the core audience? What are their concerns and values? How are they being reached today, and how will they be reached tomorrow?

2. MIDWEST VALUES – NO CONTRACT

Michael, our owner, is from Minnesota originally. The reason we bring this up is this is how we run our business. The handshake is the agreement. This is how Michael's grandfather did business and it is how he runs 51Blocks. 51Blocks does not try and lock you in for a year or even 6 months. You can leave at any point. The last thing we want is you having to do business with someone who you don't want to do business with.

3. TRANSPARENCY

We are completely transparent with all the work that we do. In your monthly reports, you will see the tasks we did the previous month and the work we are going to do in the upcoming month. We want you to feel completely comfortable with the work we are doing so you know what you are paying for.

Now that you've made it to the very end of this book, you can ask yourself if seeking a white label partner is the right option for your business. Are you ready to shortcut your path for time and financial freedom?

OUR PARTNERSHIP BENEFITS

COMPLETE PEOPLE & PROCESS MANAGEMENT

Lacking bandwidth to manage a full team and all of your clients? 51Blocks takes that out of your hands from day 1. We handle all of the client & team management to ensure you're free to focus on things that matter in your business.

COLLABERATIVE FLEXIBILITY

We're not a big cooperate structure like other providers. Our goal is to fit into your organization, not make you fit into ours. Whether you need a custom deliverable, workflow, or just have your own particular needs we're here to ensure we make it happen for you.

WHITE LABELED COMMUNICATION

We're here to operate on behalf of your agency. All of our communication systems are white labeled. We give you access to every email our team sends through our shared inbox system and provide your clients with a direct phone number to reach our team.

TURNKEY AGENCY STRUCTURE

As soon as you make a sale, your 51Blocks team is ready to go. Each partner gets operations, management, and team support to take care of your client from onboarding all the way through day-to-day fulfillment. You're welcome to be as involved or hands off as you want to be!

INDUSTRY EXPERTS

We're all about putting the right people in the right seats. This comes in the form of our specialized strategists. We understand the importance of connecting with a client through industry expertise. Individuals on our team have their own niche areas of marketing experience to provide your clients with the best strategy & ROI.

SCALABLE SOLUTION

We ensure our team is never overloaded in their own workloads so you can have the fastest turnaround when you're ready for us to execute. Whether you have a few or many clients ready to go we can generally kick things off with your core team in one business day after proposal acceptance so you can get back to selling.

White Label Partnership

Readiness Checklist

How ready are you for a white label partnership? Timing is everything when it comes to building a new relationship so you can focus on scaling. Walk through our checklist below and find out!

Yes	No	Defined Need
		Have you clearly defined the need that is driving your agency interest in white labeling?
		Is building a white label partnership an appropriate strategy to address your agency's need?
Yes	**No**	**Readiness for Change**
		Is now the right time for a partnership (e.g., it will not compete with other major changes currently being made within your agency)?
		Will your agency's leaders support change and effort required to implement and sustain a partnership? It is essential that the leaders within your organization actively support and champion your partnership.
Yes	**No**	**Time, Resources, Personnel**
		Will your agency provide sufficient support for the partnership needs to flourish and thrive cohesively with your mission?
		Will your agency require new deliverables or

Yes	No	
		provide training for current deliverables you require to be fulfilled from your new team?
Yes	**No**	**Sustainment for Change**
		Will your agency be willing to be flexible to allow a partner to continuously improve processes to support your clients (e.g new tools, deliverables, etc)?
		Will your agency be able to remain collaborative as new needs arise from each client for the benefit of retention and customer service?

Number of Yes responses you have selected is 6-8 out of 8:

This is likely a good time within for your agency to use white label services as a way to scale your agency. As you begin the implementation process, continue to monitor whether the answers to these questions change and keep a close eye on any items to which you answered "no".

Number of Yes responses you have selected is 4-5 out of 8:

Your organization may not be ready on one-third to one-half of the factors. This reduces the likelihood of partnership success. Evaluate if this is an appropriate time to participate in a new partnership or if you're just in need of additional resources to turn those no answers into yes.

Number of Yes responses you have selected is 1-3 out of 8:

Based on your responses, significant work is likely needed before your agency is ready for a partnership. Trying to engage in a partnership right now could create significant risk that it will not succeed or produce a fruitful partnership.

ABOUT THE AUTHORS

Michael Borgelt
CEO & Founder at 51Blocks

Michael started his career as a computer programmer, moved into database administration, and found a perfect match for his technical skills with internet marketing. Michael has been doing search engine optimization since...well... before it was search engine optimization. Michael was a key player in the marketing strategies behind Mortgage101.com which surged to the #1 position for the keyword "mortgage." Michael is from Minnesota originally where the handshake is the agreement. This is how Michael's grandfather did business and it is how he runs his various digital marketing agencies which includes 51blocks, a successful White Label company.

Brittany Filori
COO at 51Blocks

Based out of the Pacific Northwest, Brittany started her digital marketing career in 2012 working for a fashion website based out of Portland, where she helped to develop brand awareness & strategy for their social media presence. After obtaining her

M.B.A., she became an SEO Account Executive and has worked with every size company from large national brands to small backyard businesses. Throughout her career she has always been focused on the overarching goal of improving processes to benefit both the clients and employees alike.

For more tips & knowledge we encourage you to join our Facebook group which is exclusive to agency owners!

THE DIGITAL MARKETERS' PLAYGROUND #TDPM

facebook.com/groups/TheDigitalMarketersPlayground

Made in the USA
Middletown, DE
03 August 2022